Ebenezer S. Snell

Ebenezer S. Snell.

ADDRESSES

AT THE ANNUAL MEETING OF THE

Amherst College Alumni,

COMMEMORATIVE OF THE LATE

PROFESSOR SNELL,

Wednesday, June 27, 1877,

BY
REV. DANIEL W. POOR,
AND
PROF. WILLIAM C. ESTY.

SPRINGFIELD, MASS.:
CLARK W. BRYAN & COMPANY, PRINTERS.
1877.

LD152
.8
S6P7
copy 2

In Exch.

Amherst Coll. Lib.

Rev. Dr. Poor's Address.

Mr. President and Fellow Alumni of Amherst College, Ladies and Gentlemen:

The call of the hour is to pay our tribute of affectionate and admiring remembrance to one whom we have all known and loved, under whose instruction we the alumni have all sat, who leads our long line as the first student admitted into Amherst College, and who, after fifty-one years of faithful service to his Alma Mater, has at length gone to his reward, followed only by the pleasant recollections, sincere respect and tender regards of all who have had the happiness of his acquaintance—EBENEZER STRONG SNELL. A rare thing is it to see a person who has given the whole of a long and laborious life towards building up the institution that has reared him; but to begin one's career with the very existence of this institution, and thenceforward to identify himself with all its interests, to evince under the adverse circumstances which ever attend the founding of literary institutions, the character and scholarship, which, at the end of the third year of his graduation, warranted his being appointed Tutor, and from that moment on to consecrate himself as by a religious vow to its advancement, growing with its growth, ministering to and receiving from it strength and fame, sharing in its struggles with unrepining self-denial—never faltering in his devotion, even through protracted gloom and death-like darkness, and living on to see it emerge into assured triumph over all difficulties and all opposition, and to welcome to its festive entertainments the alumni of fifty-six classes, with all of whom he had been personally acquainted—this is the distinguishing honor which belongs to Professor Snell alone, among all we have known or read of. And how much does the mere fact thus sketched invite toward him special consideration at the very start. We cannot disparage its significance by ascribing it wholly to the mere accident of the time and place which the Professor happened to occupy. It can be accounted for only by the possession of sterling qualities not ordinarily found, and which force themselves on our notice the more, when we take into account the singular vicissitudes through which the College has passed. Mighty convulsions have shaken it to its foundations; but though they shook others out of place, they never disturbed him. In devising what could be done to make the College firmer—more popular—more effective, no patron ever thought of displacing the Professor of Mathematics and Natural

Philosophy; amid all the shakings he was one of the things that could not be shaken; and so he remained, remained on and on, until all physical vitality was suddenly exhausted, and he dropped at his post, implements in hand. We say then that Professor Snell presents himself before us in advance by the simple, obvious facts of his history as a no ordinary man. Let us then look at him a little more closely. Our part it will be, within the half hour allotted us, simply to note the main features of his history and character, as they were presented for ordinary observation. The estimate of his intellectual abilities and scientific attainments and labors, will be left to the more competent Professor who follows us.

Professor Snell was born in North Brookfield, on the 7th of October, 1801, the eldest in a family of ten children. Thus, both in the century and in the household, no less than in the College it seems to have been his fate to be at the beginning of things. One of his playful boasts was that he was born in the year *one*. His father was the Rev. Thomas Snell, D. D., pastor of the Congregational Church of North Brookfield for nearly sixty-four years. Although a trustee of Williams College, he was among the foremost to advocate the foundation of a College at Amherst, acting at first in the hope that the former institution would be transferred to the place of the latter. We remember seeing him in our early days, a clergyman of the old school, dignified and sedate, yet benign and kindly, held in high repute for his sound judgment, and for the sterling qualities of his mind and heart, eminently successful in his office—a fit type of what ministers were in the days of our fathers, when settlements were for life, and the title, Pastor, had a meaning. His wife was Tirzah Strong, a relative of Dr. Nathan Strong of Hartford, and for some time an inmate of his family. She was a woman of "peculiar mildness and affection," and proved his fit and faithful consort through nearly the whole of his long life.

Under these parents Ebenezer enjoyed a thoroughly religious training, a "blessing which," as he testifies in a brief autobiography, "can never be too highly valued," and one involving "no ordinary responsibility." He confesses to its having shaped his whole future, though he made no profession of faith until his 28th year, when, with his newly married wife, he joined the College church, March 1, 1829.

Under his father he, also, fitted for college. But since it was his purpose to enter as Sophomore, he spent one term at Amherst Academy for the sake of pursuing some studies here, that belonged to the Freshman grade. In the autumn of 1819, at the age of eighteen, he was matriculated at Williams College, then under the Presidency of Dr. Z. S. Moore. Of his scholarship some estimate may be formed from the fact that he was appointed the Latin Oration at the Junior Exhibition. At Williams he remained two years. During this period the debate waxed hot, and came to its crisis about the expediency of removing the little institution then hid away in the mountains of Berkshire, into the more level and accessible regions of Hampshire, where it would have room to grow. On this question, no doubt, the views of Doctor Snell influenced those of his son. Accordingly, when the Legislature forbade the transfer, and President Moore and others, nevertheless, adhered to their conviction of its propriety, and left Williamstown to found a college here, Ebenezer followed him with seventeen others, and having been already examined before leaving, was the first to be admitted into the new College as Senior on September 19th, 1821; and for a whole day he enjoyed the honor of being its sole student. "Pindar Field was the only classmate who accompanied him;" and these two constituted the whole class, save for a short interval, when they were joined by Ezra Fairchild of New Jersey, who however was not graduated. Alexandrians will be pleased to know that young Snell was appointed to call off the names in order of those who were to constitute their society, and was elected its first President. And here again he is at the head.

It is a noteworthy indication of the many drawbacks, against which Professor Snell achieved his education, that the winter of his Senior year was spent in teaching, first at North Brookfield, and then at Amherst Academy, as assistant to the Preceptor,

Mr. Clapp He was one of those who choose to work their way through life; and he refused to be indebted even to his father for the costs of his college course. What he did not earn he borrowed, and paid afterward. Such was the stuff of the man early developed. Beneath his slender form and retiring mien there wrought a resolute spirit, which was disciplining itself for the earnest work of after years.

In August, 1822, at the age of twenty-one, Mr. Snell was graduated—if graduation it may be called when no degree could be conferred—and at the commencement he delivered "the Salutatory," which was the highest appointment given. "It was not thought best," he writes, "to have a formal valedictory." And why not? we may ask. Was it in Providential anticipation of the fact that he was destined not to leave Amherst at all, but to abide here in constant service, until he should be called to go up higher? In a divinely ordered life, seeming chances turn to prophecies, and this appears like one. The degree of A. B., now held in reserve on the simple testimonial of worthiness, was conferred in 1825, when the college charter won from the Legislature after a hard struggle, was received by college and town in a blaze of festive illumination.

For the next three years Mr. Snell was teacher in Amherst Academy—which then held the future college, as it were, in its swelling calyx—first as assistant until 1824, then as principal for seven months after. In these positions he evinced such abilities that at the close of the summer, August 22, 1825, at the first annual meeting of the Board of Trustees under the charter, when the government of the college was regularly organized, and among other things the salaries of the officers were determined, he was chosen Tutor with a salary of $400. His old friend, President Moore, had now gone to his rest, and Dr. Heman Humphrey filled his seat; at the same time Rev. Edward Hitchcock was elected Professor of Chemistry and Natural History, and Mr. Jacob Abbott, Professor of Mathematics and Natural Philosophy; Rev. N. W. Fiske held the chair of Greek Language and Literature and Belles Lettres; Rev. S. Peck, D. D., that of Latin and Hebrew; and Rev. S. M. Worcester that of Rhetoric and Oratory and English Literature. Tutor Snell's business, it seems, was to act the part of general assistant to all these professors when need be, but especially to teach in Mathematics. At this time the students numbered 140. To the original Old South College there had been added the so-called Middle of my day without as yet the Chapel between. Thus appointed and endowed and associated, Mr. Snell entered on that career which he continued to pursue in advanced positions almost uninterruptedly for fifty-one years.

In August of 1829, Prof. Sylvester Hovey was called from Williams College to take the place of Professor Abbott, resigned; and Tutor Snell was promoted as his "adjunct," with the understanding still that he should also instruct in the languages whenever his services might be needed, and "such instruction would not interfere with the main duties of his office." From this we see how varied his attainments were, and what a valuable acquisition to the college he was through his ability to occupy several posts as occasion might demand.

In the spring of 1831, Professor Hovey went to Europe for the double purpose of recruiting his health and of purchasing additions to the Library and Philosophical apparatus. His absence left his assistant in full charge of the department until the summer of 1832, when he returned. But a brief effort at lecturing convinced him of his inability to prosecute his work, and at the following commencement he resigned his office, and Mr. Snell was at once appointed to his place. His apprenticeship had both proved his fitness and enhanced his qualifications to be Master, and he developed into the full-blown Professor as by a natural law. His first course of lectures was delivered to the then Junior class—the class of 1834—in the mathematical room where he had already arranged the Philosophical apparatus as it arrived from Paris, directing in the construction of the cases, putting in order the articles, and testing the excellence of the several instruments. So great were the improvements thus made in the department that he might be fairly called the founder of it.

The year of his appointment to the Professorship, 1833, was that in which our class entered college. We thus came under his earliest instructions. The impression he made on us then we remember well. Of a slender form, ruddy face, laughing eye and quick movement that meant business; kindly and genial in his manner, ready of appreciation and sparkling in repartee; his whole appearance toned down with something of feminine delicacy, he put all in intercourse with him at ease, and made himself popular with the students. In the Lecture Room, so far from appearing as a novice at his work, he displayed the readiness, the fullness, the accuracy, the artistic finish of a practiced instructor. It seemed as if he had been always at it. Every experiment was done to a nicety. Never was he more at home than when setting nature's forces at play, and exhibiting the beauty and exactness of their operations. They seemed, as it were, his familiars, put under a spell to do his bidding. And if ever they proved capricious, which was rarely the case, far from showing impatience, he would dismiss them with a playful jest that made up for the disappointment. Malicious students would sometimes say that the jests were prepared beforehand, and were repeated from class to class. But supposing they were, why, we ask, should not wit and wisdom be carefully wrought, and if good repeated. A great mistake is it to imagine that our best humorists never conned in advance the good things they uttered, or flung away a bright saying, simply because it pleased once. The pleasure once given is a reason for using it again. And it is one proof of our Professor's wit, that it never lost its raciness, and was entertaining to the last.

In hearing recitations Professor Snell was sharp, demanding of the students clear and definite answers. No tricks of mystification, or dodging, or saying, "That is what I meant, Sir," would avail with him. Each student was required to state precisely what he pretended to know, or there was fun in store. It is said that the now celebrated H. W. B., so noted in college days for his fondness for Mathematics! was on one occasion undergoing question amid perplexities, and thereupon helped to answer in whisper from his friend S——, who sat near. "Yes," said the quick-eared Professor, "that is S——'s view of the subject; now what is yours?" It was of no use. All H. W. B. could respond was: "I wish, Sir, you would ask S——, he knows a great deal more about it than I do."

On another occasion we ourselves, strange as it may seem, were detected smiling over a funny letter which a class-mate, now a sober D. D., had slyly passed over to us, and with shocking abruptness up we were called to state what we knew of parallactic motion. The sudden "pull up," as Tony Weller would say, so confused our wits that we were disposed squarely "to flunk," and sit down. But we were not to be let off so. The Professor was sure we knew, and he insisted on an answer. At length recollection rallied, and citing the words of the book we hurriedly replied: It is the apparent motion of objects *inter se*, (i. e.,) among themselves, we added—when the laugh of the class was brought down on us by the encouraging comment, " Very correctly translated, Sir." It was a lesson to attend to recitation a little more closely not to be forgotten.

And so it was he managed the classes. There was no acid in his composition. His correction and rebukes were all tempered with a genial humor, which allayed irritation.

In the freedom of social intercourse, his pleasantry was in constant play. He was rarely at a loss for a reply. At times his wit crackled from him quick and bright, as the sparks from one of his own Leyden jars when well charged. A touch was enough to draw him out. But the shocks were never strong,—enough to amuse, seldom powerful enough to hurt. On one occasion, when criticised for his pronunciation of acou(ow)stics as a very uncouth (uncowth) way of pronouncing the word, he replied, " O, if you take me on that ground, I will say that as for " acoostics," I do not like the soond of it, and on that accoont I shall not pronoonce it so! Rumor said that when the Tutors—shall we name them ?—W. S. Tyler, C. Park, A. Bullard, and G. C. Partridge all boarded there about the year 1836, the home at the foot of the hill resounded with the ring of happy laughters not indulged in at the regular Faculty meeting; unfortunately, however, no Gurney hid in the closet has reported the conversations which gave them birth. Perhaps one of the surviving members of that coterie might supply the lack if called upon. We would like to hear some of the good things said in those days.

Naturally, Professor Snell had an almost feminine delicacy of feeling, and the flushes on his face as they came and went, told the play of emotions that were going on within. Acts of kindness touched him to the quick, for he never was willing to believe himself as popular as he was. Very characteristic is the following incident. The class of 1858 having resolved to surprise him with a token of regard, purchased some articles of silver, and made arrangements for a formal presentation at his home by securing his being sent away on a specious errand, and getting things in readiness against his return. As he re-entered he found the whole class awaiting him. Greetings over, the class-leader conducted him to the table where stood the pieces under cover, lifted the cloth, and made his little speech. The Professor was too much overcome for a reply. After a few silent moments, relief was happily brought by a student—one of the poorest in his class—who quietly stepped up and laying his hand gravely on the Professor's shoulder said, "Now, Professor, you will understand how to sympathize with some of us when we are called upon to recite and can't." It was enough. The "over-fraught heart" was tapped, and the occasion passed off merrily. But just think of such freedom being taken with President Humphrey or Professor Hitchcock!

Thus accessible, genial, appreciative was our Professor ever. An encounter with him was a refreshment. It did the alumni good to receive from him a warm welcome on their occasional visits to Amherst, and find themselves remembered. And how racy were his little speeches at the commencement gatherings. We shall never forget the one he gave on the 45th anniversary of his graduation, when being in the chair, we congratulated the first class on all being present, and thought it fitting that we should first of all raise our Ebenezer in commemoration of the happy occasion. A pretty lively stone he proved, full of wittiest "sermon" as he repelled insinuations against his day of small things, and showed by humorous analogies how the greatest and the best ever spring from the least. And what could be more Elian in its vein than the account he gave of himself in the following year which, though no doubt remembered by all, is worth repeating. "This occasion tells me, as my friends are often telling me, that I am an old man, and I am becoming quite accustomed to the appellation. I suppose I ought to feel some infirmities, but here is just where I fail. I am not conscious of any infirmities, except the numerous ones which have always attended me. It may be supposed that I am mature enough to put on spectacles; but I do not yet see clearly any reason for so doing. And as to a cane, I have had any number of canes presented to me. The gift I always accept, but I never take the *hint*. It is possible, however, that the Sophomoric weakness may yet fall upon me, and that I shall appear abroad with all my canes at once. I perform my college work with as much ease and interest as I ever did, and really feel some solicitude lest I shall not know when to resign, unless some one tells me." O, needless solicitude! A nature so fresh could be summoned to resign only by the great Father himself.

In his habits, Professor Snell was exact, punctual, methodical. It was a question whether he went by the sun, or the sun went by him. Certainly they were often seen in close conference, and were on the best of terms. If I mistake not, he made it his business to keep the sun's accounts; and none was ever better qualified for the office. With him minutes ran golden as if each one was to be reckoned for. Yet there was no press or unseemly hurry in his movements. His life went like clock-work, "never hasting, never resting."

>Nowher a besier man than he ther n'as,
>Nor seemed he half so besy as he was.

A rare thing was it for him to be absent from his place, whether in the class-room, or chapel, or faculty meeting. Like punctilious was he in his domestic economy. Incomes and expenditures were strictly noted down, and he could tell to a dime what it cost him to live. Of all committed to his trust he was a careful steward. Obligations were by him held sacred, and were met with conscientious fidelity. His word was his bond. Yet with all this exactness he was liberal of his means when occasion called, as we ourselves can bear testimony. There was nothing penurious about him. And it was this combination of prudence with generosity which enabled him to accomplish so much for his department in preserving and increasing its apparatus on the most scanty allowances; and also manfully to endure the straitness of the many days of pecuniary embarrassments through which the college struggled. Never did a professor make a little go so far. In his report for 1843, he states that "the Philosophical apparatus has suffered no loss or damage during the past year, and has been improved by the addition of several small but valuable articles at an expense of less than $20. Perhaps an honest statement of the manner in which my time is employed for college requires me to say that most of my hours for exercise are spent in a private shop, where I construct such articles as I feel the need of in giving instruction, which lie within the limits of my mechanical ability. I estimate that the sum of $20 or $25, which is annually expended for the department, does under this economical arrangement effect an amount of repairs and improvements and additions which would in any other way cost the institution from $50 to $100." The private shop alluded to was, at first, that of Mr. David Parsons, a singular man whom we well remember, the son of Rev. Dr. Parsons, whilom minister of the parish, a genius and wit in his way, of whose skill we recollect to have heard the Professor speak in high praise. The two were much together in the early time, and a rare treat it must have been to have watched them devising and contriving to alter or manufacture on their scant allowance the apparatus which was to serve the purposes of the lecture, enlivening work with wit as they went along. Of the value of some of these inventions to science, we shall leave the Professor who follows me to speak more in full. All we can testify to is the great and well-earned pleasure he took in exhibiting his apparatus, thus revised and improved, to visitors. It was a pet he was proud of.

A marked characteristic of Professor Snell was his modesty. In early life he was diffident even to shyness. This kept him back from showing what he really was, and restrained him from pushing into positions he was well qualified to fill. His chief aim was conscientiously to discharge the duties assigned him, leaving honors, and promotions, and rewards to come as they might. Self was absorbed in work. He had devoted himself to the college, and its interests were held paramount to personal considerations. In providing for self and family, the main question was not, what do I need? or what have I earned? but what can the college afford? Likewise in his association with others, while there was an honest declaration of opinion, he never so asserted himself as to preclude harmonious co-operation. The burden put upon him, after fair deliberation, he was ready to assume and carry as well as he could. And this freedom from assumption opened him to kindly fellowship with all classes. The students approached him confidingly. The people of the town liked him as a good neighbor. Children never held aloof from him in awe. For all he had a kind word, and passed on his way leaving the impression of a sunny nature. Amherst was his home. Here he rooted himself and shook out his silver leaves to the breeze, giving a quiet pleasure to all who approached him, or sat under his shadow.

But beneath all this there were the reserved forces of a strong, self-sacrificing, resolute spirit, which came out into full exercise during the long trying season, which followed upon the great rebellion of 1837. How the college withered up and dropped both leaves and branches—and came near being cut down as hopelessly gone under the blighting influence of that hot eruption of conscience most of us have heard. Students fell off. Friends forsook. Friends failed. Debts accumulated. The treasury had not wherewith to pay the small salaries due. Applications for aid were refused. One measure after another proved abortive. People talked about the expediency of transforming the college again into an academy. It seemed as if Amherst must go down. Then it was that those who had her interests in charge showed the stuff they were made of, and the mightiness of their love. They refused to desert. They assumed the responsibility of carrying on the institution for what could be allowed them out of the pitiful income accruing from tuitions, and put their shoulders beneath the sinking fabric, strong and unbending as the Caryatides which of old upheld the temple of Diana, yet with hearts, beneath that stony firmness, which palpitated with keenest anxieties and sorrows. And among the foremost of these to do and endure was our Ebenezer Strong—proving true to his name, a veritable "stone of help" in the hour of Amherst's calamity. And here let me name the others associated with him. The noble President Heman Humphrey had been constrained to leave under the exigencies of the situation; and there remained of the old set, Professors Edward Hitchcock, (made President,) Nathan W. Fiske, William S. Tyler, Charles U. Shepard, and with these was associated Prof. Aaron Warner, recently appointed. These are the men to whose unyielding firmness and heroism, it is due that Amherst College still exists, and that we its older Alumni are not left orphans. Let us pay them honor due, and hold them in perpetual remembrance. All·now are gone to their reward, save two, and they, thank God, remain with us this day, to enjoy the happy results of that unflinching endurance. It is now forty years since the great rebellion; let us celebrate it by giving three cheers to the memory of the men that stood it through.

And brighter days came. How they came, let the history of the College so ably written by one of these men tell. Observers beholding their self-denial became friends. Donations were made. Professorships were endowed. New instructors were appointed. Building after building went up. Students flocked in. And in that glorious rising from the dust, none rejoiced more than Professor Snell. But what gladdened his heart most of all, and do you blame him? was the gift for Walker Hall. Yet, even with this, how sorely he was tried by the protracted delay in the erection of the building. For many years he had patiently endured with limited accommodations, inconvenient lecture room, and inadequate apparatus. Other colleges were striding ahead. He was getting old. And oh how he longed to put his dear College up with the best in his department, and have the pleasure of realizing his ideal before he finished his work. Once and again in his Reports, he pressed the subject on the delaying Trustees in the most respectful terms. That of 1866, he closes in the following significant strain: "Of course I would not conceal the fact that I feel a deep *personal* interest in the question, how soon the accommodations of the new building can be enjoyed by the Lecturer on Natural Philosophy? For at my time of life I can look for only a few more years at the farthest, in which to perform the duties of my present position. But this personal consideration I can sincerely say I look upon as a trifle compared with the general welfare of the College. And it is in view of the advantage to the institution, and not to myself, that I urge the speedy erection of the Walker building."

At length the goal of his aspirations was reached. Walker Hall was dedicated October 20, 1870, and happy man was he as he took possession of his spacious rooms and fine cases, and apparatus added at a cost of $3,000. No "*nunc dimittis*" does he now offer. In his Report of 1872, he writes: "Having now occupied Walker Hall two full years, I am prepared to express my entire satisfaction with the arrangements there provided. I am grateful to a kind Providence that has spared my life and health, and has permitted me to labor even for a period of two years in the convenient and pleasant quarters now furnished for the department under my care." And most heartily did all observers and listeners congratulate him on his enlargement, and wish him many days the enjoyment thereof.

And live he did four years longer, retaining marvelously his faculties unimpaired to the end. The last lecture he delivered was in the last week of his life.

Nor must I forget that Professor Snell's crowning excellence was his sincere, unfeigned piety. He did not say much about it, it is true. It was not in his nature to make a parade of anything. Indeed his diffidence was such that it was only after some effort that he could bring himself to make a profession of his faith at the age of 28, and then, after this, to take his turn in conducting College prayers. But for all this his piety was none the less sincere and deep. It pervaded his whole life, and shone out in his daily conduct. It brightened his home. It sweetened his daily intercourse. It imparted sacredness to all his obligations. It cheered him amid difficulties. It sustained him under afflictions. Twice had he been bereaved of children, and he bowed to the dispensation in Christian submission. All this was but the fulfillment of his own petition, that "the unnumbered prayers presented in his behalf by his believing father and mother might be answered, and that they might find a rich reward of their faithfulness in seeing him pursue the paths of wisdom, which they had so often pointed out to him as the ways of pleasantness and peace." Verily to him they were ways of pleasantness and peace.

Was Professor Snell then a faultless man? Theoretically he was not. No man is. But what his particular faults were we have not been able to discover. We watched him when a boy of fifteen and over. We have asked his wife and daughters, and who ought to know so well as they? We have inquired of his associate Professors. We have questioned the students and Alumni. We have ferreted among the neighbors, and we have found none willing to testify aught against him. The commendations invariably pronounced upon him have all ended without a *but*. If we were to draw inferences from what we know of his characteristic traits, we might conclude that he might possibly have been a little impatient with lazy laggards who were rarely up to time—a little tart upon irregularities of the heedless and unprincipled. We can hardly conceive of one so sensitive in his nature, and so exact with himself to be easily tolerant of traits and habits so opposite to his own. But we cannot recall or obtain instances illustrative of this. Without courting popularity it must be said that he was uniformly popular with all classes, and retained his friendships unbroken to the last. And now that he is gone, where are the lips that will pronounce aught save benedictions on his memory. Other men there have been, indeed, among us of larger dimensions, and more brilliant qualities, who have lifted themselves more conspicuously before the world's gaze; but we know of none more inviting from the simple beauty and symmetry of their character, and from their perfect adaptation to their work. His life lies before us like one of those sweet quiet landscapes, that now and then catch the eye as we sail down the placid Connecticut—where meadow, field and grove, grassy hill-side and playful rivulet combine to present a scene of cultivated loveliness, on which the mind broods with serenest satisfaction. We would not have it other than it is.

But it is time we closed our sketch. After a long and almost unbroken career of active service, toward the end of his 74th year, and on the 55th anniversary of the opening exercises of the College, September 18, 1876, Professor Snell finished his work. Premonitions of his departure were seen in fits of fainting which only interrupted for the time his regular duties. He continued to lecture up to the last week of his life, as Professor Tyler remarked in an obituary notice of him, "with his usual clearness and method, and his characteristic dexterity and success in experimental illustrations, though not with all his normal quickness and vigor." The last time was on Wednesday, September 13. On the following Monday he was gone. Only an hour before he breathed his last, as he came out of one of his fits, he said in his usual pleasant vein, "I am everywhere but here;" and to the suggestion that wherever he was the Savior was with him, he gave a pleased assent, and so took his leave, calm, peaceful, blessed.

It is but fitting that I should add to my impressions the beautiful tribute paid Professor Snell by his almost life-long associate, Professor Tyler, as it appeared in the "Amherst Student," of October, 1876, which was sent to us after most of the above was written, and fully corroborates all we have said.

"Thus the last living human link is severed, which for five years more than half a century has bound together all the years in the history of Amherst college, and united all the graduates, all the alumni and all the officers of the college to one another, and to their Alma Mater, by their common relation to this oldest son and brother. There has been no other such link, and there never can be another.

"What Professor Snell has been to Amherst College, and what he has done for it as its first student, and one of its earliest tutors and professors, more than half a century an officer of the college, and more than a quarter of a century an officer of the church, the regulator of the calendar, of the catalogue, the clerk of the bell and the clerk of the weather, the model teacher and lecturer, the exemplar of the faculty and the students, the guide, instructor, elder brother and father of us all—no son of Amherst need be told, for it is written in the history of the college and in all our memories—the memory of our hearts. And none need be told of the beauty of his character and life, for we have all seen and loved and admired his perfect integrity, his transparent purity and sincerity, his matchless modesty, his rare and rich vein of pleasantry, his gentleness tempered with firmness, his kindly sympathy towards all men, his loyalty to

God and his faithfulness in every duty; and we shall never forget it. If there is any man in the whole range of our observation and experience to whom we should dare to apply the epithets, blameless and faultless, I think we should all agree that that man was Professor Snell."

Professor Esty's Address.

PROFESSOR SNELL AS A TEACHER AND A SCIENTIFIC MAN.

IN such a life as Professor Snell's there is much to satisfy our idea of completeness. His uninterrupted career of more than half a century of successful labor, —his long-continued influence for good, exerted upon more than fifty successive college generations, are elements of this completeness. His life was complete in its resources, in its happy combination of congenial and satisfying pursuits. "To pass our time in the study of the sciences," says Lord Brougham, "has in all ages been reckoned the most dignified and happy of human occupations." But Professor Snell had a two-fold resource. He had a love of mechanical pursuits, together with an ample opportunity for its exercise in the field of his professional work. Next to congenial intellectual labor, indulgence of mechanical skill, guided by intellect, and inspired by love, is most absorbing and satisfying. Professor Snell possessed the resources of the student of science and of the artist. In addition to this he was a teacher, and he had the instinctive love of a true born teacher for his work. But it is mainly because of his Christian character, ripened by experience and perfected by time, that we speak of his life as a completed, rounded life, and symbolize our thought by the sheaf of ripened wheat. We find on closer examination, these more immediate and apparent elements of completeness are but the appropriate setting and expression of the inner principle of his mental life.

The primary instinct of his mind was an impulse to the attainment of completeness in some practical, tangible form in all he did. It was the key to his character. It was the secret of his method. It explains the peculiar excellence of his teaching. It was the basis of his intellectual tastes. It was the inspiration of his faithfulness. It was the life of that higher, though unconscious, tuition whose lessons are among the most valuable acquisitions of the past. He had the instincts of the natural mechanic and artist. He loved good and genuine workmanship. He loved a neat and finished product. He loved simplicity, harmony and beauty,—directness and economy of means. The unfinished, the uncouth, and slovenly jarred upon his artist nature as discord upon the soul of the musician. His eye kindled with enthusiasm over a piece of superior workmanship as over an intellectual achievement. His hand and eye were trained by skillful manipulation in the practical mechanics of the workshop, and by the habit of exact and delicate experiment. Patience and care, exactness and aptitude, are the natural products of such a discipline. A tendency to the attainment of a perfect work is engendered and strengthened by a long-continued course in such pursuits.

But while this tendency to the attainment of an exacting conformity to an ideal was thus strengthened by the practical discipline of the workshop, the influence of his intellectual studies was in entire consonance with that of his practical pursuits. What John Stuart Mill says of the physical sciences in general, applies with particular force to Natural Philosophy: "Its whole occupation consists in doing well, what all of us, during the whole of life, are engaged in doing, for the most part badly." Natural Philosophy is the product of perfected human thinking. It exhibits in its perfected form, the working of the scientific method. "It is the Principia of Newton," says Stanley Jevons, the logician of science, "it is the Principia of Newton that is the true Novum Organum of modern science, and not the method of Bacon." The central method of the Principia, as also of modern science, consists of the interaction between hypothesis and experiment, through deduction. Where has hypothesis been so daring and yet so fruitful, where has deduction been so profound and subtile, and yet so sure, and experiment so refined and ingenious as in Natural Philosophy? The method of Natural Philosophy gives us the model, not only of scientific, but of all exact thinking. The habits of mind engendered by long-continued occupation with this method, we should expect would exhibit something of the peculiarities of the discipline by which they are formed. We should expect a distaste for loose, indefinite, and unfounded thinking. We see in this method the secret of Professor Snell's caution, wariness, and especially what Faraday particularly emphasizes as the effect of a study of Physics, "good judgment, reservation of opinion, a mind open to conviction, resistance to self-deception, habits of forming clear and precise ideas, imagination under control, labor of thought, and humility." He was thus, on the practical and theoretical side of his nature, habituated to the comparison of his work with a high standard, with a perfect ideal, a habit of mind conducive on the one hand to superior attainments, and on the other to self depreciation.

Both these elements, the discipline of the workshop and of the study, so distinctly marked, so easily traced, blended generally in the way of mutual modification and restriction; but in this particular, in this stimulation of the impulse to work out a completed product, they coincided in their effects, and intensified each other. The effect of this two-fold culture upon the primary instinct of his character to perfect whatever he undertook was, of necessity, a restriction of the field of his activities in some directions, and an extension in others. The restriction was mainly on the scientific side, as the extension was on the artistic. The practical element was the controlling one. In the union of the two elements in his character as a teacher, this was noticeably the case. This impulse on its practical side became, under the demand of teaching for expression and interpretation, a source of artistic power, and of an artistic habit of mind.

In its most elementary form this artistic habit was manifest in his love of orderly arrangement, of having a place for everything and everything in its place. In his lectures he always proceeded according to a definite and well tested plan. He never assumed anything. Everything was tried, tested and recorded. He never trusted himself, but arranged and noted beforehand, the time, place, and performance of every piece in the combination to be produced. He was therefore seldom taken by surprise,— seldom failed in an experiment. In its merely mechanical arrangements, each lecture proceeded with the smoothness and freedom of a frictionless machine. In his diagrams, charts and models, he exhibited another element of the artist nature, not only in his painstaking fidelity to truth as far as possible, but in the mechanical execution in the interests of neatness and beauty.

It was, however, as an interpreter of scientific

truth that he exhibited in perfection those characteristics which I have ventured to call artistic. He made the interpretation of abstract truth an art. Here he showed inventive talent, ingenuity in the adaptation of means to an end, a control over the materials at command, and power over mechanical combinations, which, when exerted for the purpose of conveying or revealing truth, are among the higher elements of artistic power. "It is the office of Art," says Hazlitt, "to combine general truth with individual distinctness." Not only definitions, new terms, technicalities were associated with some concrete object, with some striking experiment, or with some familiar fact that gave precision and definiteness, but also the generalizations of science, the abstract statements of scientific hypothesis were conveyed by some ingenious illustration by which the imagination was quickened—the meaning apprehended—the principle grasped, with all the distinctness of immediate vision.

This inventive art is most clearly seen in the design and construction of his ingenious pieces of apparatus for illustrating the different varieties of wave motion. They are among the most successful products of a teacher's art. The doctrine of wave movements in different media is an important part of modern physics. Deep down into this almost impenetrable rock the physicist has pushed the mighty instrument of modern analysis, and has established the fact that in this direction lies the secret of a most important and recondite part of natural phenomena. The treasures gathered in this search are among the most brilliant gems in the crown of analytic genius. It is of importance that in a course of education which ought to involve at least an outline of what mind has done with the intractable mysteries which surround it, it is of importance that the student should have a clear conception of the hypothesis that unlocks so many secrets. This is successfully accomplished in the pieces of apparatus to which I have referred. The conceptions that lie hidden in the analytic formulæ of Cauchy and Fresnel are here brought to light in a material form, and are made real and vivid, so that one of the most difficult, as it is one of the most important generalizations of science, is made by this art one of the most clearly apprehended theories of scientific thought.

This impulse to work out a completed result in the simplest and most economical way exhibited itself in the daily drill of the recitation room. It made him seem sometimes exacting and particular. It was not easy to satisfy a man who combined in himself the logical rigor of mathematics, with the artistic sense of the perfect. Slipshod work, vague notions, hazy generalizations, superfluous and lumbering circumlocutions were the special abhorrence of this master workman. It was, therefore, one of his peculiar excellencies as a teacher that he held before the mind of the student uniformly and persistently the exact and exacting standard of precise thinking. For this art the methods of Physics furnish the model, and Professor Snell was so thoroughly imbued with their spirit that he brought them to bear in full force upon the mind of the pupil. The student was sure to get the full benefit of what Dr. Whewell puts forth as the crowning excellence of the English University training—what he designates as "practical teaching," leading the pupil to clear ideas of fundamental truth, and above all, to a practice in the deductions to be made from them.

The revision of Professor Olmstead's text books in Natural Philosophy and Astronomy was carried out with a view to this kind of teaching. They are clear, logical, carefully divested of all redundancy, and expressed with precision and care.

The impulse to the attainment of a finished product manifested itself in his intellectual tastes. It led to the study of truth in its detailed and individual relations and applications. It was the *Art* of mathematics, rather than the *Science*, which he loved. His favorite branch of mathematics was Descriptive Geometry. He preferred graphical methods to deductive analysis. He loved the special forms, the isolated and elegant constructions, the simple and individual methods of the Greek geometry rather than the more general and subtile methods of modern analysis. Harmony and simplicity of relation in individual forms were to him elements of beauty in mathematical truth as they were to the old masters of Geometry. We have an illustration of this in his published propositions relating to the sphere, and one of the circumscribed cones, whose properties fairly rival those of the famous sphere and cylinder of Archimedes. In this way his artistic tendencies modified and shaped his scientific tastes. They prescribed the form under which he looked upon scientific truth. And thus we find in the form of his art the indications of the limits imposed upon his science. Whatever the hand could trace, whatever the eye could see, whatever mechanical skill could reproduce or embody, formed the material of his scientific thinking. Abstraction and generalization had little interest for him except in so far as they admitted of concrete embodiment, of individual and special realization. It was to this individual, practical method of viewing truth that he owed his great success as a teacher and interpreter of science. It was the basis of his art of interpretation. It was the key by which he gained access to many a mind otherwise hopelessly closed to the appeals of exact science.

The counterpart of this method is that of the modern analytic treatment of Physics which lies outside the province of general college instruction. The secret of its power is in the fusion of exact experiment with the profound deductions of modern mathematics. Within its limits it realizes the true conception of a Natural Philosophy. It is an organic system of thought underlying the phenomena of Nature. It is an evolution of thought through the sure though subtile transformations of the analyst from the fundamental principle up to its countless concrete realizations. In the mystic symbols of its written language we read the history of universal movement as the mysterious ebb and flow of that energy it has brought to light. And this method also has its art which does not depend on the eye. In contrast to the plastic art of the special method I may call it the poetry or the music of science, because like its analogue in esthetics, it appeals to the spirit without the intervention of material forms. Its appeal to the enthusiasm of its votaries is through the grandeur of its combinations, not only in their majestic sweep through space and time, but in the unity and harmony of their all-embracing comprehension.

That science has such an esthetic province, is contrary to the great authority of Goethe, who says: "the antipodes of poetry is not prose but science." But Sir William Rowan Hamilton, the greatest analyst of the last half century, the peer of Newton and La Place, as well as universal genius, said: "The 'Mecanique' of Lagrange is a poem." The poet Wordsworth, the friend of Hamilton, said of Hamilton's own achievements of constructive imagination in the forms of pure analysis, that they entitled him to admission within the charmed circle of poets. One of the most eminent of living mathematicians says of a particular development of modern analysis: "It is the music of reason." We may also recall here Plato's profound definition of beauty as "the splendor of the true."

The fundamental law of Prof. Snell's mental life was to attain the goal of a tangible product complete in all its details. It determined the direction of his scientific thinking. It manifested itself in his practical nature—in his practical culture, and in his intellectual tastes. The instinctive love of the perfect was also the basis of his esthetic tastes, and of his religious aspirations. All his susceptibilities were tuned in harmony with the benign influences of the true, the beautiful, and the good. He was a man

"Feelingly alive
"To each fine impulse, with quick disgust
"From things deformed, or disarranged, or gross"

To his associates, co-laborers and pupils, he manifested this instinct in the scrupulous attachment to principle, in the fidelity to truth which characterize the science he loved. In his straight and even course—in his untiring faithfulness to duty, he embodied the very spirit of truth' and duty. These traits were ever tempered by his geniality, kindness and simple-heartedness.

He loved a completed work. In all these long years of faithful service, there was an unseen artist moulding his character. A master-workman, whose nature it is also to do all things well. This artist has finished his work. He has taken it hence. But it lives in our memories as an untarnished Christian life.

0 019 629 459 4

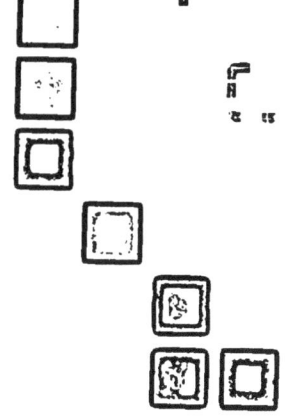

CPSIA information can be obtained
at www.ICGtesting.com
Printed in the USA
LVHW080017240922
729062LV00033B/103